LUNCH BOX NOTES

>> for <<

COURAGEOUS
Girls

**Make lunchtime
fun AND inspiring!**

Published by Shiloh Kidz, an imprint of Barbour Publishing, Inc., 1810 Barbour Drive, Uhrichsville, Ohio 44683, www.shilohkidz.com

Our mission is to inspire the world with the life-changing message of the Bible.

Member of the
Evangelical Christian
Publishers Association

Printed in China.
000977 1221 HA

LUNCH BOX NOTES
for
COURAGEOUS
Girls

Make lunchtime fun AND inspiring!

SHILOH kidz
An Imprint of Barbour Publishing, Inc.

*"Be strong and courageous!
Do not be afraid or discouraged.
For the L*ORD *your God is with
you wherever you go."*

JOSHUA 1:9 NLT

Roses are red,
violets are blue,
out of all the courageous
girls in the world,
I'm so glad I have you!

*"The Lord your God is
the One Who goes with you.
He will be faithful to you."*

DEUTERONOMY 31:6

make today a fun day!

☐ Be silly with your friends.

☐ share a favorite joke.

☐ use your imagination!

The loving-kindness
of God lasts all day long.

PSALM 52:1

I know it's only lunchtime,
but I just want to say—
I can't wait to see you
and hear about your day!

*"For the LORD your
God is going with you!"*

DEUTERONOMY 20:4 NLT

you are

- ☐ funny
- ☐ fashionable
- ☐ pretty
- ☐ talented
- ☐ smart
- ☐ all of the above!

*We can trust
God that He will do
what He promised.*

HEBREWS 10:23

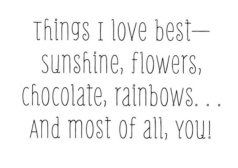

things I love best—
sunshine, flowers,
chocolate, rainbows. . .
And most of all, you!

*Everything you do
should be done in love.*

1 CORINTHIANS 16:14

you are so talented!
I love watching you

☐ make music
☐ draw
☐ sing
☐ dance
☐ _____

"*Do not be afraid or troubled. Be strong and have strength of heart.*"

JOSHUA 10:25

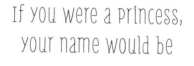

If you were a princess,
your name would be

_____

_____,

because _____

_____

_____

_____

_____.

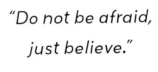

"Do not be afraid,
just believe."

MARK 5:36

GOOD JOB!

I KNEW

you

could do it!

I can do all things because Christ gives me the strength.

PHILIPPIANS 4:13

when i think about you,
my heart

☐ smiles
☐ does a happy dance
☐ feels all cozy
☐ _____

Be strong with the Lord's strength.

EPHESIANS 6:10

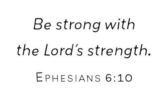

A lunchtime laugh
from me to you...

Knock, knock.
Who's there?
Wilma.
Wilma who?
Wilma lunch be ready soon?

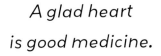

A glad heart

is good medicine.

PROVERBS 17:22

I hope you enjoy
your lunch today!

I packed it with

LOTS OF LOVE!

*My help comes from
the Lord, Who made
heaven and earth.*

Psalm 121:2

Forget about yesterday.
(And remember that
I love you!)

I know that everything God does will last forever.

ECCLESIASTES 3:14

I am thinking about  today...

and I know you will do a terrific job (because you're one terrific girl)!

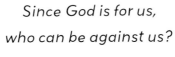

Since God is for us,

who can be against us?

ROMANS 8:31

My favorite time of the day...
is the time I get to spend with
my favorite girl!
(And that would happen to be you!)

With God's help we will do mighty things.

Psalm 60:12 nlt

someday I think
you'll be a famous

☐ movie star   ☐ artist
☐ dancer   ☐ musician
☐ author   ☐ _____

*(No matter what you choose
to be when you grow up,
you'll ALWAYS be a star to me!)*

"Have strength of
heart and do it."

Ezra 10:4

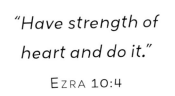

Thank you for:

_____
_____
_____
_____
_____
_____
_____
_____.

You are one special girl!

"I have told you these things so you may have peace in Me. In the world you will have much trouble. But take hope! I have power over the world!"

JOHN 16:33

I know today
hasn't been the best,
but always know that

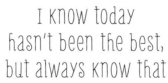

I BELIEVE
IN YOU!

"I am the Lord your God
Who holds your right hand,
and Who says to you, 'Do not
be afraid. I will help you.'"

ISAIAH 41:13

It's Friday!

Let's plan something fun
together for the weekend!
what will it be?

☐ a trip to a museum

☐ a manicure and pedicure

☐ an all-night movie
marathon

☐ _____

Our hope comes from God.
May He fill you with joy
and peace because of
your trust in Him.

ROMANS 15:13

we go together like

☐ popcorn and a movie

☐ peanut butter and jelly

☐ cookies and milk

☐ _____

Let us go with complete trust to the throne of God. We will receive His loving-kindness and have His loving-favor to help us whenever we need it.

HEBREWS 4:16

I am your biggest fan because:

_____

_____

_____

_____

_____

_____,

YOU
ROCK!

There is no fear in love. Perfect love puts fear out of our hearts.

1 JOHN 4:18

today, I hope you notice

☐ the sunshine

☐ how special you really are

☐ how good it feels to be a great friend

☐ how much you are loved

☐ _____

☐ all of the above

*"Do to others as you would
like them to do to you."*

LUKE 6:31 NLT

In case I haven't thanked
you yet today for being
such a great kid,
consider this an official
"Thank You"
from my heart to yours!

Christ in you brings hope of all the great things to come.

when I think about you,
my face looks like this:

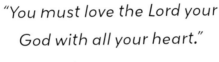

"You must love the Lord your God with all your heart."

LUKE 10:27

unscramble the words below
for a special message.
UOY ERA USOUCERAGO!

___ ___ _____!

(Yes, you are!)

Wait for the Lord. Be strong.

Let your heart be strong.

Yes, wait for the Lord.

PSALM 27:14

make today a great day!

- ☐ listen to your favorite song.
- ☐ sit with your best friend at lunch.
- ☐ give your teacher a compliment.
- ☐ remember that i love you!

"The Lord is my Helper.
I am not afraid of anything
man can do to me."

HEBREWS 13:6

If I were a queen, I'd be

_____

_____.

And you'd be my princess,

_____

_____.

What great
royalty
we'd make!

"I am the Light of the world. Anyone who follows Me will not walk in darkness."

John 8:12

just a little reminder from me:

_____

_____

_____

_____

_____

_____

_____.

Praise the Lord, O my soul.
And forget none of His
acts of kindness.

PSALM 103:2

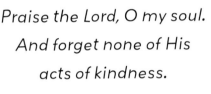

A little humor to
brighten your day...

voted most likely to
succeed in school:
porcupines—they're sharp.

"He will yet fill your mouth
with laughter and your lips
with shouts of joy."

JOB 8:21 NIV

you are so good at:

I am
wowed
by you!

Learn to pray about everything. Give thanks to God as you ask Him for what you need.

Philippians 4:6

If we had a theme song,
I think it would be:

☐ "I love you, you love me"

☐ "Girls Just Wanna Have
Fun"

☐ "These Are a Few of My
Favorite Things"

☐ _ _ _ _ _ _ _ _ _ _ _ _ _ _ _ _

Trust in the Lord with all your heart, and do not trust in your own understanding.

PROVERBS 3:5

great job on:

_ _

_ _

_ _

_ _

_ _

_ _

_ _

_ _.

you worked so hard!

I will sing to the Lord, because He has been good to me.

Psalm 13:6

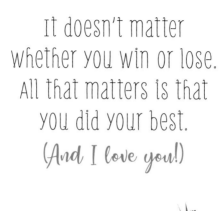

It doesn't matter
whether you win or lose.
All that matters is that
you did your best.

(And I love you!)

*Return to the
Lord your God,
for He is full
of loving-kindness.*

JOEL 2:13

If at first you don't succeed,
try, try again!

I am so proud of you
for trying!

Follow what is good.

3 John 11

special thoughts to carry
with you all day long:
You are special.
You are loved.

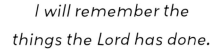

I will remember the things the Lord has done.

P SALM 77:11

Sending you
some sunshine
on this cloudy day!

"Learn to do good.
Look for what is
right and fair."

Isaiah 1:17

surprise!

Enjoy this special little treat
I packed just for you—
my favorite girl!

*I will give honor
and thanks to the Lord,
Who has told me what to do.*

PSALM 16:7

Knock, knock.
Who's there?
Lettuce.
Lettuce who?
Lettuce dig in and eat!

I hope you enjoy
your lunch today!

For You have made me glad by what You have done, O Lord.

PSALM 92:4

If you have any worries today, think about

- [ ] summer break (it will be here before you know it!)
- [ ] the weekend (we'll do something fun together!)
- [ ] the bell ringing at the end of the school day
- [ ] recess!

For the Lord God helps Me.

Isaiah 50:7

when i think about you, i

- ☐ smile
- ☐ giggle
- ☐ feel all warm and fuzzy
- ☐ am proud as a peacock
- ☐ _____

You are living this

new life for God.

ROMANS 6:11

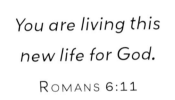

Let's celebrate you tonight!

How about:

- ☐ an outing to the park
- ☐ ice cream cones and you and me!
- ☐ dinner out—you choose the place

can't wait for our special time together!

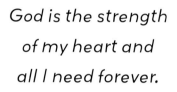

God is the strength of my heart and all I need forever.

PSALM 73:26

If I could send you a butterfly
or rainbow just to show you
how much I care, I would.
Instead, I'm sending you this
little note to tell you how
much you are loved.

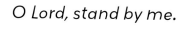

O Lord, stand by me.

PSALM 26:1

unscramble the words below
for a special message.

HVEA   A   TRGEA   AYD!

_ _ _ _   _   _ _ _ _ _   _ _ _!

God is our safe place and our strength. He is always our help when we are in trouble.

PSALM 46:1

Here's lunch (and a laugh)—
packed with love
from me to you!

Knock, knock.
who's there?
Wayne.
Wayne who?
Wayne are we going to eat?
I'm starving!

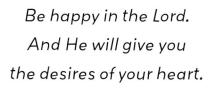

Be happy in the Lord.
And He will give you
the desires of your heart.

PSALM 37:4

Today, I hope you remember
to be thankful for

☐ your family

☐ good friends

☐ your favorite teacher

☐ a delicious lunch packed
by yours truly!

"The Lord will always lead you."

Isaiah 58:11

If all of the girls in the
universe were lined up and
I could choose only one,
I'd choose YOU!

"I will trust and not be afraid. For the Lord God is my strength and song."

ISAIAH 12:2